Maxwell Eaton III

BEAR GOES SUGARING

NEAL PORTER BOOKS

HOLIDAY HOUSE / NEW YORK

EEE·KEE·SIE

With special thanks
to Dr. Joseph Orefice of the Yale School
of Forestry and Environmental Studies

Neal Porter Books

Text and illustrations copyright © 2019 by Maxwell Eaton III

All Rights Reserved

HOLIDAY HOUSE is registered in the U.S. Patent and Trademark Office.

Printed and bound in September 2019 at Toppan Leefung, Dong Guan City, China.

The artwork for this book was created with watercolor and graphite pencil

on 140 lb. bright white, cold press, watercolor paper.

Book design by Jennifer Browne

www.holidayhouse.com

First Edition

1   3   5   7   9   10   8   6   4   2

Library of Congress Cataloging-in-Publication Data

Names: Eaton, Maxwell, author, illustrator.

Title: Bear goes sugaring / Maxwell Eaton III.

Description: First edition. | New York : Holiday House, [2019] | "Neal Porter

Books." | Audience: Ages 4-8. | Audience: K to grade 3.

Identifiers: LCCN 2019010708 | ISBN 9780823444489 (hardcover)

Subjects: LCSH: Maple syrup—Juvenile literature. | Sugar maple—Juvenile

literature. | Cooking (Maple sugar and syrup)—Juvenile literature. | LCGFT: Picture books.

Classification: LCC TP395 .E28 2019 | DDC 664/.132—dc23

LC record available at https://lccn.loc.gov/2019010708

WARNING!

Making maple syrup involves drills, heavy buckets,
fire, stoves, and boiling liquid. Please do not attempt
without the guidance of a responsible (human) adult.

I'm forty-two in dog years.

The winter has been long and cold, and while the temperature is still below freezing at night, it's now above freezing during the day. The sun is shining, and spring is on its way. It's sugaring time! Time for Bear to make maple syrup.

Sugaring Time

—Starts between mid-February and early March
—Nights in the 20s °F
—Sunny days in the upper 40s to low 50s °F
—Ends by early April when nights get warmer

First, Bear gathers her tapping supplies.

BRACE
A hand-powered drill

Bear could use a power drill if she preferred.

7/16-INCH DRILL BIT
Attaches to brace and drills the perfect-sized hole for Bear's spouts. Other spouts may need a 5/16-inch bit instead.

Bear is ready to tap! But she needs to find a certain kind of tree.

Maple syrup is mostly made with the sap of the sugar maple tree. It can be difficult to identify in the winter when there aren't leaves on the trees, but Bear planned ahead and marked her sugar maples with ribbon tape in the fall.

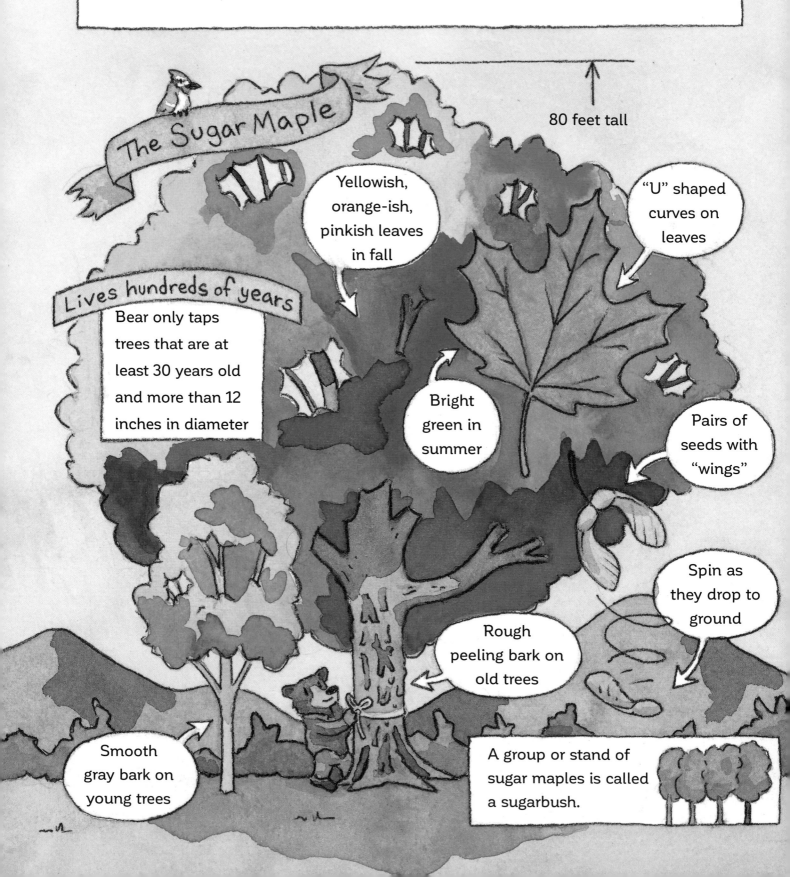

There are a few other types of maple tree where Bear lives in the cold northeast. She could tap those as well, but they have less sugar in their sap.

Bear has found her sugar maples. She begins tapping by drilling straight into the tree about two feet above the ground.

How are those pancakes coming?

A piece of tape tells Bear when the hole is 2 inches deep.

2 feet

Inside the tree

Outer bark protects the tree
Inner bark transports nutrients

Sapwood (or xylem) transports sap
Heartwood gives the tree extra support

Annual rings—one for each year the tree is alive

After drilling, Bear places a spout into the hole and taps it lightly with a hammer until it's firmly in place. She is careful not to hit it too hard, which could crack the wood, or too light, which might not hold the weight of a bucket of sap.

Bear remembers to place the hook on the spout before hammering.

Finally, Bear hangs a bucket from the spout and puts a cover on top to keep leaves, bark, insects, rain, and snow from falling in.

All summer long, leaves make food for the tree in the form of sugar.

Sugar →

Sssup

The leaves fall in the autumn and this sugar is stored inside the limbs, trunk, and roots.

Hey!

FFFT!

The tree then rests for the winter.

Z

Ack!

WHUMP!

Spring comes and freezing nights cause gases and sap in the tree to shrink, which pulls water in through the roots. The water mixes with stored sugar to form more sap.

The next day, as the temperature rises above freezing, the gases and sap expand and build up pressure inside the tree, like air in a bicycle tire.

I left the bottle right here.

Tapping the tree is like slowly letting a little air out of the tire. Only, instead of air, it's sap. And it's being caught in a bucket.

This cycle of freezing and thawing is what causes sweet sap to flow each day during this special time in the spring. It's why we have maple syrup.

Aaah.

Drip drip drip

CRCKS

There it is.

Who is that?

The trees are tapped, and the sap is running. Bear needs to put together her evaporator.

Turning watery maple sap into sweet maple syrup involves one main thing: evaporation. When a pot of water is boiling on a stove, the hot water turns from water (liquid) into steam (gas). The water evaporates, and soon there's nothing left in the pot!

The same goes for sap. Only when the water turns into steam, it leaves sugar behind. Boil off enough water, and you're left with thick, sugary maple syrup.

Since maple sap is only two to three percent sugar, it takes a lot of boiling to get rid of enough water. If Bear starts with forty gallons of sap, she'll have to boil off thirty-nine gallons of water to be left with one gallon of maple syrup. Yikes!

To do this quickly, Bear will need an evaporator, which is simply a shallow pan with an intense source of heat. Here's how she builds it . . .

The Evaporator

Bear stacks cement blocks in a "U" shape with an old stovepipe at the end to act as a chimney. (In a pinch, she could skip the chimney and simply leave the ends open.)

I feel like we're getting away from pancakes and syrup here.

But enough about buckets and holes.

A chimney helps to channel heat and smoke from the fire like a hole in a bucket channels water.

Then she places a large, flat, shallow pan over the cement block "arch." This will hold the sap. (Bear doesn't use a pan that anyone will miss.)

Now you're stacking logs?

Focus on the pancakes, please.

Last of all, Bear stacks some wood nearby. It's from a fallen tree that she cut and split last summer. She also stacks downed branches she's been collecting. It will all be needed to keep a fire burning under the pan for an entire day.

Bear is ready to go!

All week, Bear collects her buckets of sap and pours them into covered, food-safe buckets in a cool and shady place. Once she has forty or fifty gallons, it's time to boil!

Bear could boil with much less sap if she needed to. It all depends on the number of taps, type of evaporator, and Bear's schedule.

Do most breakfasts take a week to make?

So... hungry.

RSSHH

Sometimes Bear finds ice in her buckets. If it's just a piece, she tosses it on the ground. It's mostly frozen water, and Bear is after the sugary unfrozen sap left behind. Though if the bucket is frozen solid, she keeps it.

Early one morning, Bear fills the evaporator pan with sap. Then she makes a fire underneath with some newspaper, dry twigs, and a few small logs. She adds more and more logs to get the fire nice and hot.

Wake up. Something is happening!

Z

Finally!

With sap warming over the fire, steam starts to rise. That's maple syrup being made!

As water evaporates, Bear adds more and more fresh sap so that the pan doesn't empty and burn. But instead of adding buckets all at once, she props up a can with a hole in it on the corner and keeps it full of sap as it drains into the pan. This is called a pre-heater.

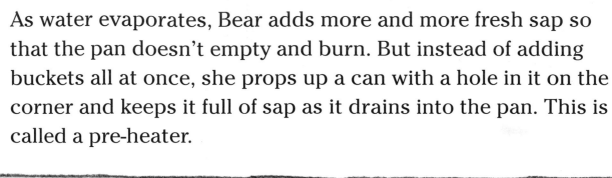

So now holes are a good thing?

Like drips from a tap, this little stream of sap fills the pan as quickly as water is boiled off.

Pre-heater (old can)

Bear uses a kitchen strainer to skim scummy foam that floats at the edges of the pan. She simply tosses it in the snow.

Right behind you.

Bear wears leather or rubber gloves to protect her paws from hot drips and steam!

Bear spends all day tending the fire, adding sap to the pre-heater, and skimming foam until her buckets of sap are empty and the maple syrup is almost done.

Bear checks to see if she has syrup the old-fashioned way. She dips a spatula into the boiling sap and pulls it out again. If the sap comes off in drips, it's not ready. If it slides off in wide sheets or "aprons," it's syrup.

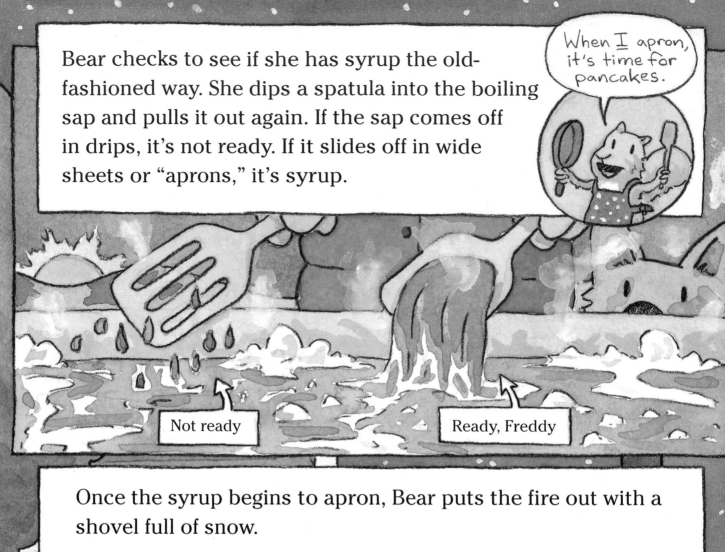

Once the syrup begins to apron, Bear puts the fire out with a shovel full of snow.

If she wanted, Bear could stop right here, but she wants to make sure the syrup is perfect.

With the fire now out, Bear carefully (CAREFULLY!) ladles the pan of hot syrup through a coffee filter and into a big pot. Looks like she's got about a gallon!

Bear takes the pot of syrup into the house to finish up.

Inside on the kitchen stove, Bear brings the syrup back to a boil. This time she uses a candy thermometer to tell her the temperature of the syrup. When it reaches 219 degrees (F) (seven degrees higher than the boiling point of water where Bear lives), she'll officially have maple syrup.

Candy thermometer

At this stage, Bear is watching for boil-overs where the syrup suddenly bubbles out of the pot in a hot and sticky mess. When she sees it happening, she simply flicks it with a few drops of cream, and it goes down.

Look! The syrup is 219 degrees (F)! Bear turns off the stove and ladles the finished maple syrup into perfectly clean canning jars. Of course, she sets a small glass aside to cool for a taste of this gift from the trees.

Bear puts the full jars on their sides, so that the hot syrup will sterilize the insides of the lids.

Delicious! All of that hard work was worth it. And before the sugaring season is out, Bear will have enough pure maple syrup to last her all spring, summer, fall, and winter.

How much does she eat?

Now what?

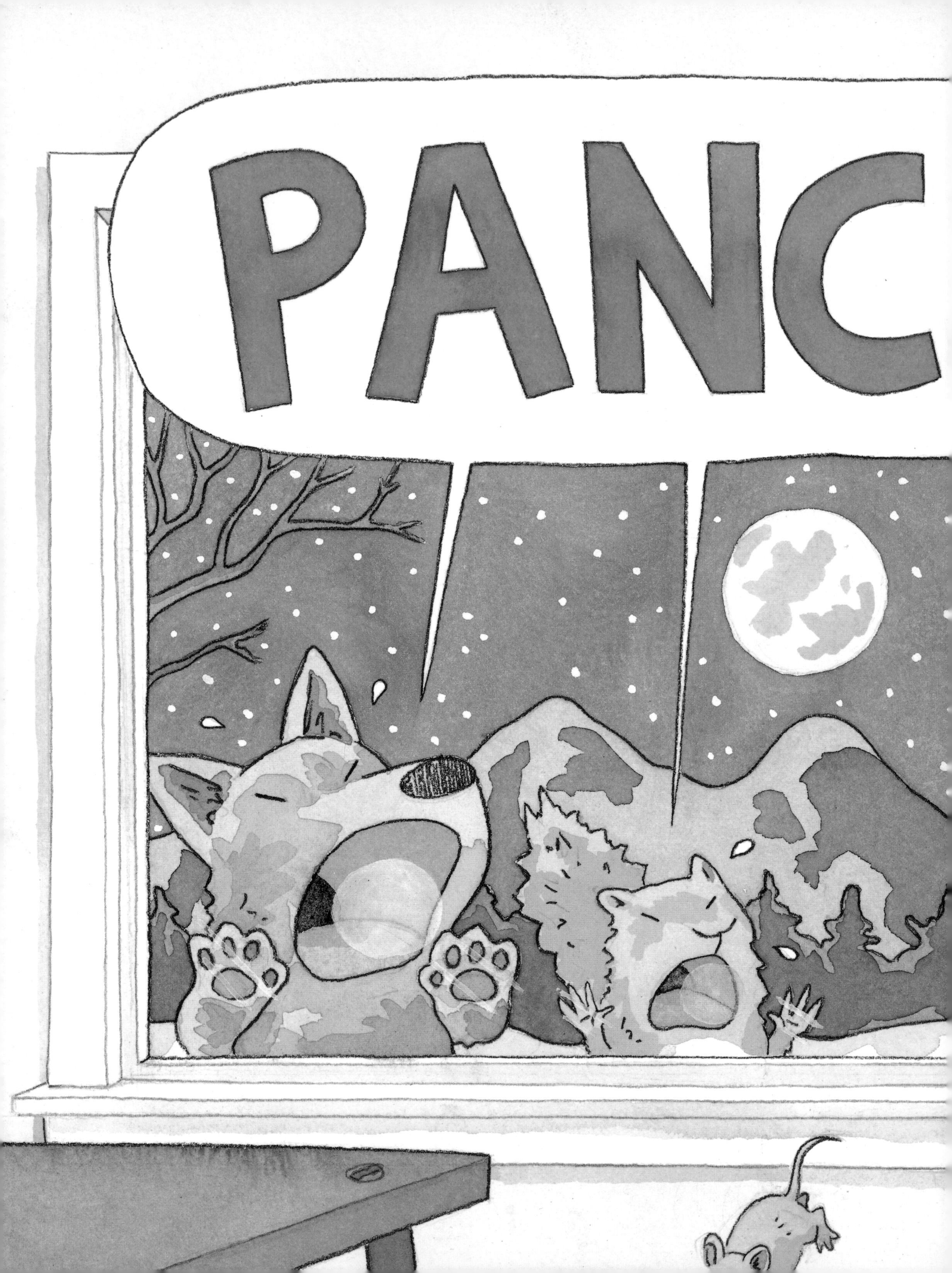
PANC

Mmm . . . maple syrup splendor.

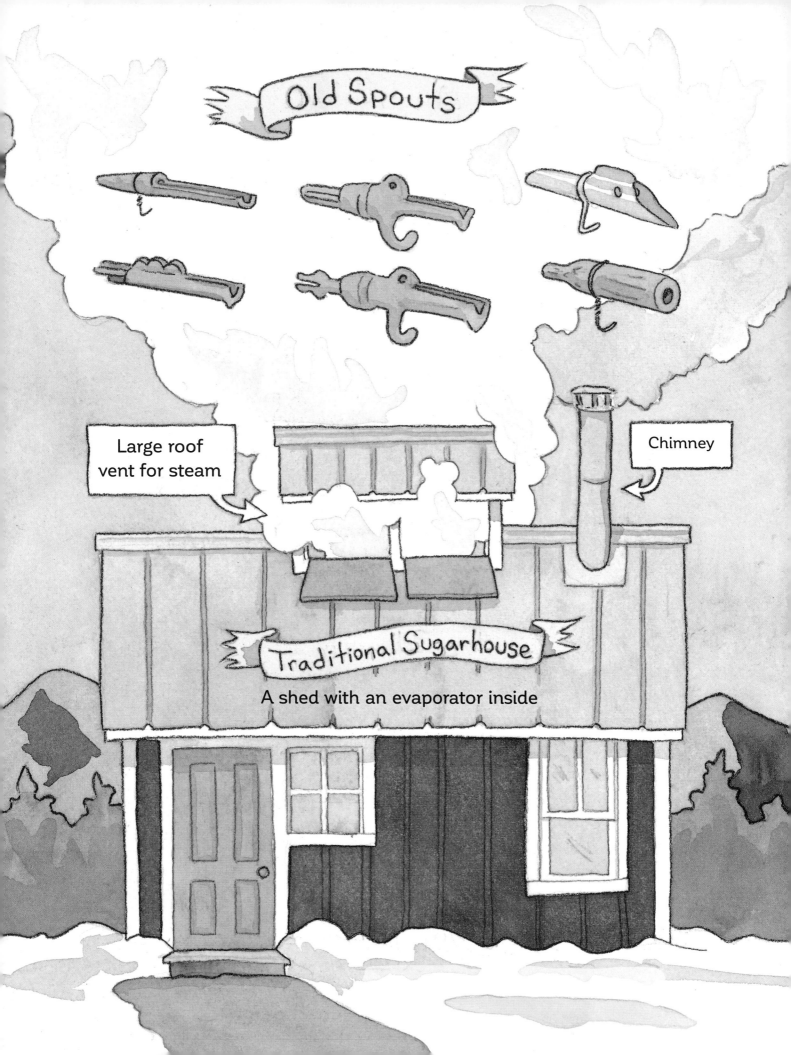

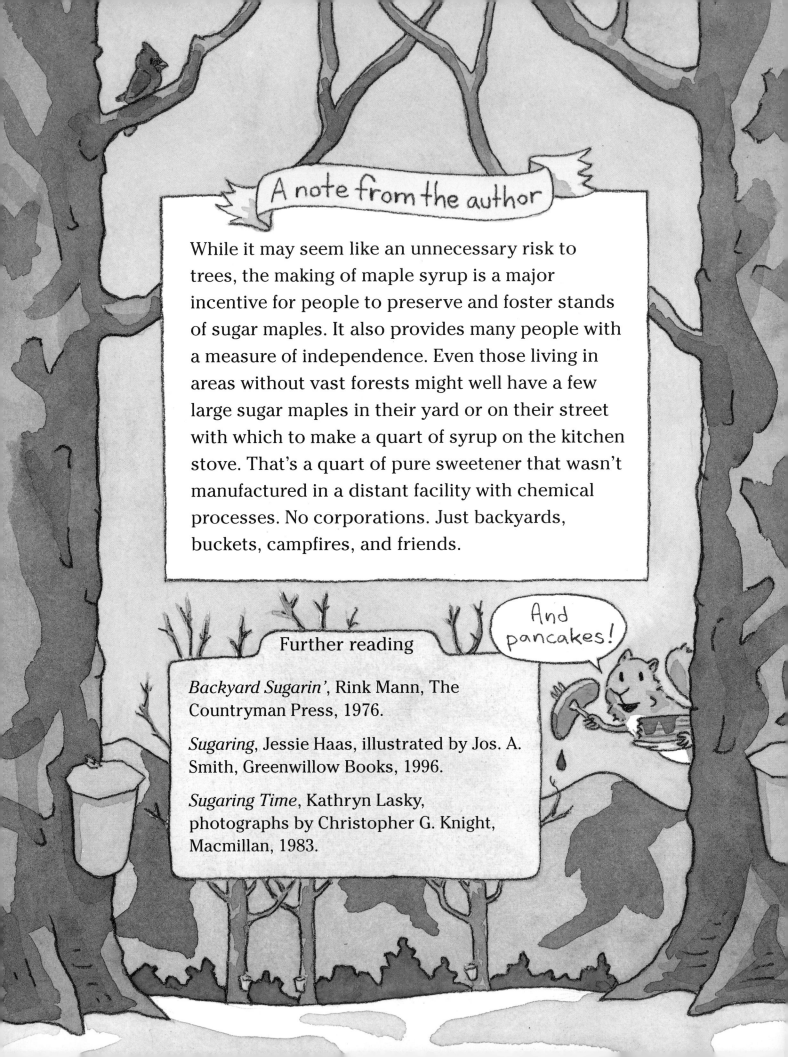

A note from the author

While it may seem like an unnecessary risk to trees, the making of maple syrup is a major incentive for people to preserve and foster stands of sugar maples. It also provides many people with a measure of independence. Even those living in areas without vast forests might well have a few large sugar maples in their yard or on their street with which to make a quart of syrup on the kitchen stove. That's a quart of pure sweetener that wasn't manufactured in a distant facility with chemical processes. No corporations. Just backyards, buckets, campfires, and friends.

Further reading

Backyard Sugarin', Rink Mann, The Countryman Press, 1976.

Sugaring, Jessie Haas, illustrated by Jos. A. Smith, Greenwillow Books, 1996.

Sugaring Time, Kathryn Lasky, photographs by Christopher G. Knight, Macmillan, 1983.